THE BOWES MUSEUM

The Bowes Museum

Elizabeth Conran, Bryan Crossling,
Howard Coutts, Joanna Hashagen, Sarah Medlam

SCALA BOOKS
Published in association
with The Bowes Museum

© The Bowes Museum 1992
Barnard Castle
County Durham DL12 8NP, England

First published 1992
by Scala Publications Ltd
3 Greek Street
London W1V 6NX
Distributed in the USA and Canada by
Rizzoli International Publications, Inc.
300 Park Avenue South
New York
NY 10010

ISBN 1 870248 93 7

Designed by Alan Bartram
Edited by Paul Holberton
Photographs by Jim Kershaw, Mike Smith,
Eddie Ryle-Hodges and Gordon Coates
Produced by Scala Publications
Filmset by August Filmsetting, St Helens, England
Printed and bound by Graphicom, Vicenza, Italy

The following organizations have assisted with the
purchase of a number of The Bowes Museum's
acquisitions included in this book:
National Heritage Memorial Fund: p 27.5; p 48.1;
p 49.3; p 69.2.
Victoria and Albert Museum Purchase Grant
Fund: p 27.5; p 31.4; p 35.3; p 36.1; p 48.1; p 49.3;
p 52.3; p 54.2; p 55.4; p 60.3; p 69.2; p 70.2; p 74.1;
p 95.4.
National Art Collection Fund: p 31.4; p 36.1; p 37.4;
p 37.7; p 48.1; p 49.3; p 54.2; p 60.3; p 69.2; p 74.1.
The Friends of The Bowes Museum: p 27.5; p 31.4;
p 36.1; p 37.4; p 37.7; p 48.1; p 49.3; p 51.3; p 54.2;
p 55.4; p 60.3; p 69.2; p 70.2; p 74.1; p 95.4.
Pilgrim Trust: p 36.1.
ICI: p 36.1.
Hadrian Trust: p 69.2.
Rothey Trust: p 69.2.
Mr S. Pratt: p 74.1.

SPONSORED BY   ENGLISH ESTATES
The Bowes Museum is administered by
Durham County Council

Contents

The Bowes Museum (South Front,
*c*1985)

The Bowes Museum

Barnard Castle is a small country town in the hills of Northern England. At its core is a Norman fortress from which the town takes its name. Its streets retain their medieval plan, though they are now lined with seventeenth- and eighteenth-century houses. Above the stone roofs and smoking chimneys descending to the River Tees, there are glimpses of green fields and trees and of dark hill ridges beyond.

Leaving the town centre by Newgate (new in 1800), the curious visitor will come to a park, follow a high wall topped by mature trees, turn into a smart entrance gate – and into another world. Set against the sky, full-face to the midday sun, sprawls a huge French château in its formal garden. This is The Bowes Museum.

It is a complete shock. Oblivious to its neighbours in scale and style, it is nevertheless triumphantly successful by its very difference. It sparks that same electricity as the Pompidou Centre in the Place Beaubourg in Paris.

The association of Paris and Teesdale, coupling the exotic wider world with long continuity from the past, describes the character and purpose of The Bowes Museum, and reflects the origins of its founders, John and Josephine Bowes.

The Bowes family came to Teesdale following the Norman Conquest. Their founder was a relation of the Earl of Richmond, himself a relation of William the Conqueror. By a succession of judicious marriages over several centuries, the Bowes came to own large tracts of land in the counties of Durham and Yorkshire. Their principal residence was Streatlam Castle, two miles from Barnard Castle. The Bowes family excelled in military, legal, administrative and political work, always as servants of the Crown. Their lands contained coal seams, and they were at the forefront of developments in the mining and transport of coal in the North of England from the seventeenth to the nineteenth centuries. They loved horses, the theatre, gardening and building. In 1767 the sole heiress to this family history and wealth, Mary Eleanor Bowes, married John Lyon, ninth Earl of Strathmore. The couple's eldest and third sons were successively tenth and eleventh Earls. It is from the eleventh Earl of Strathmore that Her Majesty Queen Elizabeth The Queen Mother, Patron of the Friends of The Bowes Museum, is descended.

John Bowes, born in 1811, was the illegitimate but fully acknowledged and much loved son of the tenth Earl, who married the boy's mother, a Teesdale girl called Mary Millner, the day before his death, in an attempt to secure his son's succession. Two very public court cases did secure for the nine-year-old boy the Bowes estates in County Durham, but kept him on the fringes of the society he was educated to enter. After studying at Eton and at Trinity College, Cambridge, where he made friends with the novelist William Makepeace Thackeray and A. W. Kinglake, author of *Eothen*, John Bowes stood for Parliament in the first post-Reform Bill election in 1832, and was elected Liberal MP for South Durham. For the next fifteen years he was active in Parliamentary and public affairs and pursued his own interests as landowner, industrialist (coal and shipping), race-horse breeder and art collector.

Bowes began collecting paintings at the age of nineteen, in the tradition of the English *milordi*, on his first visit to the Continent. The paintings he chose were mostly the kind fashionable in the 1830s and '40s, Italian Renaissance and Dutch seventeenth-century works. However he did show an individual and advanced taste for that time in buying a group of fifteenth-century works from Italy and Northern Europe (Section 1). Besides Old Master paintings, Bowes commissioned portraits of his best horses and brood mares from John Frederick Herring senior, and later from Harry Hall and Thomas Bretland. Racing was a lifelong passion. The Streatlam Stud, founded by the tenth Earl of Strathmore, never had more than ten brood mares at one time, but such was the judgement of Bowes and his trainer, John Scott, that he bred four Derby winners in twenty years. The last of these, West Australian, was the first ever winner of the Triple Crown in 1853. These achievements place Bowes amongst the most successful owners in British racing history.

In 1847 Bowes gave up Parliament and moved to an easier social life in France. Always attracted to the theatre, and to the ladies of the theatre, Bowes purchased the Théâtre des Variétés on the boulevard Montmartre, Paris. Almost immediately he formed a liaison with Mlle Delorme, an actress in the theatre company, whose actual name was Benoîte-Joséphine Coffin-Chevallier. Soon she was installed, with John Bowes's support, at 7, cité d'Antin (today the headquarters of the French Rugby Federation) playing the role of patron of the arts as well as her roles on stage. Her portrait by Tony Dury, painted in 1850 when she was twenty-five, demonstrates that she was interested in artistic patronage from early adulthood. She is surrounded by the furnishings of her new home. Beside her on a table are the scripts of plays commissioned by herself as star vehicles. While the portrait was in progress, she was appearing in *Pomponette et Pompadour*, a musical comedy in which a poor village girl (Josephine) impersonates the marquise de Pompadour, mistress of Louis XV, and one of the greatest patronesses of the eighteenth century.

In 1852 John Bowes took the unusual step of marrying his mistress. His wedding present to her was the Château Du Barry at Louveciennes, once the gift of Louis XV to another of his mistresses, the comtesse Du Barry. (By 1852 the seventeenth-century château and the eighteenth-century Pavillon Du Barry were separate properties.) The Bowes totally refurnished the château in the latest styles, with the assistance of the Parisian firm, Monbro fils aîné. In 1855 they moved their town house from cité d'Antin to 7, rue de Berlin (now rue de Liège)

and refurnished again. Later, some of the finest pieces from these refurbishments
were retained for The Bowes Museum. Today they form the core of its
important collections of French nineteenth-century decorative arts (Section 6).

Josephine Bowes's interest in the visual arts was even greater than her love for
the theatre. She was a talented and dedicated painter, and throughout her life
continued to develop her technical skills, scale and colour harmonies, in response
to the avantgarde of the 1850s and '60s. By the late 1860s she was exhibiting
regularly at the Salon. The Bowes Museum owns about sixty works by Josephine
Bowes, most of which are landscapes (p. 81).

As a result of Mme Bowes's interest in modern art the collection has about 150
works by sixty-seven French artists born between 1800 and 1830. Collected from
the 1850s to the early 1870s, they demonstrate the interest then current in
subjects from modern life, both people and their environment. There are
landscapes of the Île de France and Channel coast, scenes of everyday life in the
city and the country, and portraits or depictions of events of immediate historical
interest. The most advanced works are by Courbet and artists associated with
him (Section 6). Although Josephine Bowes must have seen early works by the
Impressionists, exhibited in the same Salons as her own paintings, these artists
were all younger than her. She bought few paintings by artists born after 1830.
Her appreciation of modern art seems to have stopped with artists of her own
age.

John and Josephine Bowes had no children, to their regret. Perhaps the
decision to found the Museum arose from this gap in their lives, as well as from
a desire to be a patron (on Josephine's part) and to commemorate the Bowes

name (on John's part). (After the latter's death the Bowes estates would be
merged with the patrimony of the Earls of Strathmore.) The initiative came
from Josephine Bowes. In 1862 she sold the Château Du Barry and devoted the
proceeds to creating the Museum. Several small plots of land were purchased to
form one large plot of nearly twenty acres, on the outskirts of the town of
Barnard Castle. The family home of Streatlam was nearby and could provide
stone from its own quarries, which was a considerable saving.

While the land was being assembled, the building was commissioned from
Jules Pellechet, a French architect whose family firm had worked for the Bowes
in France. Pellechet liaised with John Edward Watson, an English architect who
had worked for the Bowes at Streatlam, and who would supervise work on site.

Pellechet looked to Continental museums for inspiration, particularly to
nineteenth-century French museum design. This reflected the origins of French
public collections – the châteaux which had employed so many artists, and
whose contents were pillaged to form public collections after the Revolution in
1789. Napoleon I had inaugurated a programme of new museum provision
throughout France in the early years of the nineteenth century, and this style of
museum became a model. (In contrast, contemporary British museum design
reflected the antiquarian and naturalist interests of their founders, who were
frequently learned societies or individuals, educated in the classics and interested

in systematic classification. Their ideal architectural form was a Greek temple, dedicated to the Muses.) The foundation stone was laid by Josephine Bowes on 27 November 1869, with the words, 'I lay the bottom stone, and you, Mr Bowes, will lay the top stone'. The building was not topped out until after her death.

Purchasing for the museum began about 1861-62 and continued until about 1875. John Bowes made a clear distinction between his family inheritance and what he and his wife had bought personally. All works of art belonging to the Bowes family were given to his Strathmore relatives, with the addition of his racing pictures. Family items that are now in the museum have entered the collection since the 1920s.

The Bowes's policy was largely educational. They wished to introduce the wider world to the people of Teesdale and the North of England, by presenting as wide a variety as possible of materials, techniques, objects and artists. The choice of objects was enormously wide – paintings, sculpture, miniatures, prints, ceramics, glass, metalwork, furniture, clocks and watches, automata, *objets d'art*, objects of vertu, tapestries, embroideries, antiquities, geological specimens, books and manuscripts, architectural woodwork. The same wide policy applied to countries. At first they contemplated world coverage, but eventually reduced their scope to Europe. Every country forming Europe in 1870 is represented in the collections.

The launching of the S.S. John
Bowes from Palmer's Yard, Jarrow,
30 June 1852, from the *Illustrated
London News*, 10 July 1852

With regard to named artists, they preferred to buy one work by each of
several artists than to buy several works by one major artist. This policy can be
seen in their purchase of Spanish paintings from the collection of the Countess
de Quinto. Indeed in buying from this collection it is revealed that they were
prepared to set aside personal taste in favour of public education. 'Although these
two [Goya and El Greco] do not appeal to you as masters', wrote their agent,
Benjamin Gogué in 1862, 'I think you might well take one of each of them for
your collection', and they took his advice. Works by the greatest artists may be
few, but there are very many signed works by lesser names, the quality of which
is nevertheless very good. The Bowes's collection is one where looking at the
object is more important than looking at the label.

Study of the history of paintings was already well developed by 1860. Study of
the decorative arts was in its infancy. The Bowes did not advance the collecting
of, say, furniture or silver, but they did bring a new range to the collecting of
ceramics and textiles, certainly in a British context. Josephine Bowes took a
European view of ceramics in the 1860s, before Lady Charlotte Schreiber began
her pioneering activity in the same field. The textile collections cover six
centuries and every kind of non-industrial technique. They included more than
sixty large tapestries and over seven hundred embroidered or tapestry chair
covers (now reduced to some four hundred by the sale of 'duplicates', *ie* the
breaking up of sets, in the 1920s).

Two important factors governed the Bowes's collecting activities – time and
price. They had set themselves an extraordinary task, to fill a huge building,

Château Du Barry, Louveciennes, 1862, in a photograph by Pierre Rion of Versailles (dates unknown)

equivalent to a municipal museum, in a comparatively short time. John Bowes was fifty years old when the museum project began. Josephine Bowes was thirty-six. They had to buy quickly, in quantity. To do this they had to buy cheaply, and they needed help.

They may not consciously have set themselves a price limit, but in practice they were buying most items for under £10, and very few for more than £100. Since many of their purchases were made in Paris, the collection offers some idea of what was available at the lower end of the market in that city in the 1860s. Very many objects were still available following the upheaval of the French Revolution in the 1790s, and more emerged in the wake of the Franco-Prussian War in 1870 (Sections 4, 5). Low prices rarely reflect high fashion. But high fashion often becomes highly unfashionable. The long-term result of buying at low prices is a collection which has weathered one hundred years of changing taste remarkably well. What the Bowes purchased still forms a very high percentage of what is on view today. Their instinctive choice is now supported by research, leading to a greater appreciation of 'minor masters' and a greater recognition of major masters in the decorative arts.

It is amusing now to see what was then low fashion – El Greco at £8, Courbet and Fantin-Latour at £4, Boudin at £2, Sassetta (then ascribed to Fra Angelico) at £6.75. The lowest individual price that has been found is 35 centimes, approximately one pence (Section 6). At that time 25 francs equalled £1 or $5.

To collect in quantity at speed required assistance. In every sphere of activity, be it estate management, industrial development, racing or collecting, John

Bowes had an ability to choose expert assistance to carry out his wishes. His agents in collecting were Benjamin Gogué, a Parisian art dealer and picture restorer, and three other Parisian dealers, M. Lamer, Mme Lepautre and M. Basset. They also bought regularly from M. Briquet, a jeweller in Paris, and M. Rogiers, a dealer in Ghent. Many items were bought in London, and on foreign tours. A store, workshop and accommodation were built at 29, rue Blomet in Paris to house the growing collection before shipment to Streatlam, pending completion of the Museum.

John Bowes was a careful recorder of all his activities. Once again he distinguished between Bowes family affairs and the Museum. Records of the building and collections, and other aspects of his life in France, are deposited in the Museum, and provide a rich source of information on the collections.

In 1869 the Bowes came to England to lay the foundation stone. They were still there when the Franco-Prussian War broke out (July 1870), which was followed by the Commune, preventing their return to Paris until October 1871. During the latter stages of the war the Prussians besieged and bombarded Paris. A shell landed in the garden at rue Blomet, just missing the museum store. The starvation and anxiety suffered by the inhabitants of Paris may have contributed to the death of Benjamin Gogué in March 1871. Josephine Bowes's health, never robust, went into a decline with worry. Although building and collecting continued briskly, she never recovered her strength. She died in Paris in February 1874 at the age of forty-eight. Her death was a great blow to her husband. It had been a particularly happy and fulfilling marriage. Conscious of his own age (he was sixty-three), John Bowes soon gave up collecting altogether and concentrated entirely on building and administrative matters. These were many – cataloguing, packing, shipping, conserving, displaying and future financing. When John Bowes died in 1885 the task was inherited by trustees. They needed courage, for Bowes's estate was not finally settled for twenty years. In spite of these enormous difficulties, the public opening of The Bowes Museum was carried out on 10 June 1892.

The trustees were empowered to add to the collections, but had few resources. As a result, the art collections were not developed beyond the founders' lifetimes. Since it would now be impossible to make up lost ground, art collecting has been restricted to the founders' period of interest, the fifteenth to the nineteenth centuries. The trustees chose to develop local history and antiquities collections and to create a useful reference library on local history, at a time when the town had no public library. The foundations of British decorative arts, toys, costume and quilt collections were also laid at this time (Section 7).

By the early 1950s mounting expenses and reduced investment income almost brought about the closure of the Museum. However, so strong was public feeling

Visit by Her Majesty Queen
Elizabeth The Queen Mother on
the occasion of the formal transfer
of The Bowes Museum by the
Trustees to Durham County
Council, 1 November 1956

that it should be saved, that a solution was found. Trusteeship was transferred by
the Minister of Education to Durham County Council. The formal ceremony
took place on 1 November 1956 in the presence of Her Majesty Queen Elizabeth
The Queen Mother. In 1949 she had supported the formation of the Friends of
The Bowes Museum to help save the Museum, and in 1962 she graciously
agreed to become their Patron. She has always taken a close and constructive
interest in the Museum's welfare.

Under Durham County Council the Museum has had a new lease of life and
has gained a larger public. The County Council has undertaken major building
repairs and vital improvements (such as electric lighting in the public galleries!).
Staffing has expanded, to include a staff picture restorer (from 1957) and
designer (from 1960), far-sighted appointments in those days. The most
important change in display policy was to create a series of period rooms on the
first floor following the example of the Victoria and Albert Museum in London.
A series of French rooms in the 1960s was followed by an English series in the
1970s, while single-subject displays were renewed. A small annual purchase fund
has been supplemented by very generous grants from national organizations and
the Friends, as well as by some public appeals. This has enabled the Museum to
acquire some outstanding items which expand, sharpen the focus, or lift the
quality of the founders' collections. Another important source has been

allocations by HM Government of works accepted in lieu of capital transfer tax. The Museum is regarded as the next most important collection of European decorative arts in Britain after the Victoria and Albert Museum. Acquisitions concentrate on European art, though fine objects from Britain are also acquired. Many British acquisitions have a North of England or Bowes family provenance. The Museum has also been enriched by many smaller gifts of costume, quilts, toys and local antiquities, which have enabled new areas of specialization to develop.

The Bowes Museum is the result of the vision, generosity and abilities of two people, John and Josephine Bowes. They created in fifteen years what any large city would be proud to offer as the product of generations of civic patronage. This vision has been preserved and enhanced by Durham County Council. The collections offer a comprehensive and educational survey, yet remain personal and quirky. Their European dimension is even more pertinent today as the Museum enters its second century. The pages that follow will present a collection which is unstereotyped, full of quality, enjoyment and humanity.

Not all museums lift the spirits. The Bowes Museum certainly does. That first impression at the entrance gate, so unexpected and magnificent, is not betrayed inside. It is the entry to another world of experience.

ELIZABETH CONRAN
Curator

The Bowes Museum (Entrance
Hall, *c*1910)

1 The Fifteenth and Sixteenth Centuries

John Bowes's interest in paintings is first recorded during his travels on the continent in 1830. He visited museums in Brussels and Antwerp, and a collection offered for sale at Aix-la-Chapelle. In the same year he purchased a *Temptation of St Anthony* by Cornelis Saftleven, still in the Museum. He is not known to have bought further Old Master paintings, through auction or from the dealer Edward Solly, until 1840. Some he bought then can now be recognised as copies of masterpieces in other collections by, say, Raphael and Tintoretto. However, others are important. A 'Fra Angelico' has since been identified as a predella panel from the polyptych painted by Sassetta for the Guild of Wool Merchants' chapel in Siena in 1423-26. A triptych by the Master of the Virgo inter Virgines is the largest known work by this artist, famous for his powers of expressing grief (p. 19). *The Rape of Helen* from the circle of Primaticcio (p. 27) is the most important School of Fontainebleau painting in Britain. Other purchases of that time include a Salviati from the Orléans collection, and paintings by Solario (p. 22), Girolamo da Santa Croce and Caprioli, as well as Northern European works now attributed to Schauffelein, Oostsanen and Benson. While Bowes 'missed' in buying High Renaissance works he 'scored' in buying fifteenth-century and Mannerist works. At that time neither artistic period was given separate status and fifteenth-century works were dismissed as primitive. Bowes collected sufficient to be considered an early enthusiast.

In 1862-63 the Bowes acquired some paintings from the collection of the Countess de Quinto, which had been formed in Spain after the dissolution of the monasteries in 1835. It included paintings by Spanish, Italian and Flemish masters. Among the sixteenth-century Spanish paintings are works by Juan de Borgoña and artists from the circle of Sánchez Cotán, as well as the passionate *St Peter* by El Greco, today the most famous painting in the collection (p. 23). Other purchases at this time included works from the circle of Bernard van Orley, and by Vincenzo da Pavia, Gossaert and van Heemskerck.

Sculpture seems never to have been a strong interest of the Bowes, but the Museum shows several fine small-scale pieces of the Renaissance period, including the Nottingham alabaster (p. 21), the marble relief of Mars by Mosca (p. 22) and several good carvings from Northern Europe. The Museum's collection continues to grow and its modern role as a regional centre for archaeology and local history prompted the acquisition of the Monk Hesleden relief (p. 21).

As early as 1840 John Bowes was also showing some interest in wider fields of collecting, when he bought the woodwork from Wren's Temple Church in London. During the 1850s the Bowes paid lip service to the fashion for Gothic or Renaissance interiors only in the reproduction furniture they bought for their homes, but immediately they began to collect for the Museum, they turned to the period itself. One of their first museum purchases was the carved and painted altarpiece by the Master of Ste-Gudule (p. 20). This was bought from the 1859 sale at auction of the stock of Monbro fils aîné (who had until then only provided domestic furnishings for the Bowes) for 1,500 francs (£60).

The collections of Renaissance decorative arts are not large, but contain rare and interesting pieces. In the field of ceramics, the finest pieces of maiolica were already commanding high prices by the mid-nineteenth century and this may have deterred the Bowes who were always careful purchasers. However there are a few charming pieces of maiolica, including the Deruta dish showing a schoolboy (p. 25). The Bowes also collected small groups of the fashionable German stonewares, Palissy ware and individual pieces such as a sixteenth-century French earthenware salt of architectural form, with a marbled glaze. Gothic stained glass was already expensive, but later, predominantly small-scale panels were collected, particularly of German or Swiss glass (p. 25). There is a small group of illuminated manuscripts and early printed books with fine bindings.

Of the important tapestry collection several pieces date from the fifteenth and sixteenth centuries. The earliest is a Franco-Flemish Gothic tapestry of about 1500, representing Spring. Other important pieces are a fragment from the *Triumph of Time* series woven in Brussels in about 1507 for Philip of Cleves and bearing his coat of arms, and two Alsatian panels after Dürer's woodcuts of the *Life of the Virgin*. The Bowes collected a number of ecclesiastical textiles, mainly fragments from vestments, including an interesting group of fifteenth-century German orphreys. A small group of domestic embroideries includes a valance of c1580 (p. 26).

Master of the Virgo inter Virgines (active *c*1475–*c*1500)
Dutch
Centre panel of a *Crucifixion* triptych, 1490s
Oil on panel, 218.8 × 196.3 cm
Founders' bequest; inv.no. 168

1

1

1

nish

arpiece of *The Passion, Death*
l Resurrection of Christ,
460-c1480
ak, and oil on panel,
41 × 568.5 cm
Founders' bequest; inv.no. W.123/
1018-1023
The painted panels of this
altarpiece are from the workshop
of the Master of the View of Ste-
Gudule. The oak centre-piece was
carved in Brussels: it is punched in
three places with the image of a
mallet, one of the marks of the
Brussels Guild of Sculptors.

2

**Stefano di Giovanni called
Sassetta (1392-1450)
Italian (Siena)**
A Miracle of the Eucharist,
c1423-c1426
Tempera on panel, 26.7 × 40.6 cm
Founders' bequest; inv.no. 52
A Carmelite laybrother, about to
receive communion sacrilegiously,
has been struck dead. The
consecrated Host is bleeding,
indicating perhaps that the
laybrother had doubted the real
presence of Christ in the Eucharist.
Sassetta's skill in creating
architectural space is evident even
on this small scale, and can be
compared with Florentine
experiments with perspective of
this date.

3

English
Christ's Descent into Limbo or *The
Harrowing of Hell,* 15th century
Detail of a carved relief of *The
Passion and Death of Christ,* from
a church (now demolished) at
Monk Hesleden, County Durham
Stone, height of detail 57.8 cm
Donated 1968; unnumbered

4

English (Nottingham?)
The Baptism of Christ, late
15th century
Alabaster, height 55 cm
Founders' bequest; inv.no. S.122

2

3

4

1

2

3

1
Giovanni Maria Mosca (active 1507-1573)
Italian (Padua)
Mars, 1520s
Marble, height 33 cm
Founders' bequest; inv. no. X.12

2
Andrea Solario (*c*1460-*c*1520)
Italian (Milan)
St Jerome in the wilderness,
*c*1510-15
Oil on panel, 69.8 × 54.3 cm
Founders' bequest; inv.no. 42

3
Spanish
St Sebastian, dated 1523
Silver and silver-gilt,
height 26.2 cm
Founders' bequest; inv.no. X.4597

4
**Domenikos Theotokopoulos
called El Greco (1541-1614)**
Spanish (Toledo)
The Tears of St Peter, signed,
1580s
Oil on canvas, 108 × 89.6 cm
Founders' bequest; inv.no. 642
Painted in the 1580s, this is the
first of several versions of the
subject by El Greco. It came from
the collection of the Conde di
Quinto and was purchased
reluctantly by John Bowes in 1869
for 200 francs (about £8). El
Greco's work was little appreciated
at the time.

1

**Maerten van Heemskerck
(1498-1574)
Dutch**

*An Allegory of Innocence and
Guile*
Oil on panel, 92.7 × 70.8 cm
Founders' bequest; inv.no. 624
This is a personification of Christ's
injunction to the Apostles in
Matthew 10:16, 'be ye therefore
wise as serpents and harmless as
doves'. The studied pose and
stylish dress of the figure is typical
of a Northern artist's assimilation
of Italian Mannerism. Formerly
attributed to the School of
Fontainebleau.

2

German (Lower Saxony)
Embroidery, late 14th/early
15th century
Silk on linen, form of darning
stitch, painted outlines,
111 × 112 cm
Founders' bequest; inv.no. Emb.384

3

**Possibly by Michael Müller of
Zug (died 1582)
Swiss**
Panel of stained glass, inscribed
'Jos Bürgi Stadt- und Landweibel
der Grafschaft Toggenburg/
1568' (Joss Bürgi, town and
country bailiff for the country of
Toggenburg), 33 × 22 cm
Founders' bequest; inv.no. SG.1
Such small panels were made by
stained glass painters for secular
use after the Reformation.

4

Italian (Deruta)
Dish, *c*1550
Tin-glazed earthenware, painted
in colours, diameter 36.5 cm
Founders' bequest; inv.no. X.1517

1

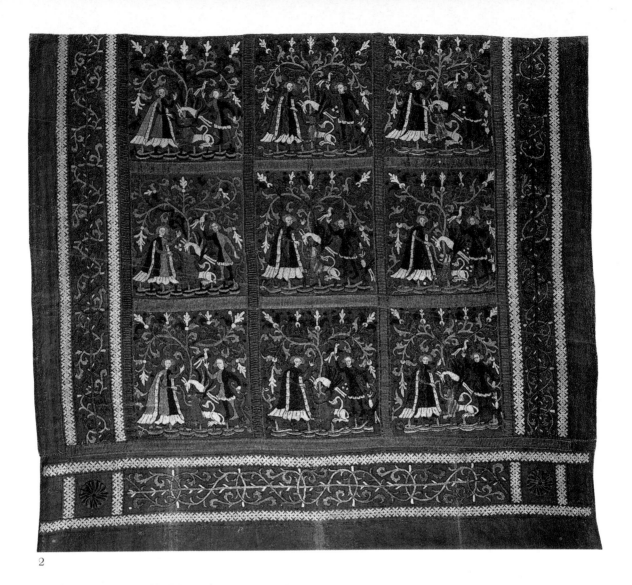

2

3

4

1

2

1
Follower of Bernard Palissy
(1510-1590)
French
Moulded dish, *c*1600
Earthenware, painted in coloured
glazes, width 28 cm
Founders' bequest; inv.no. X.1556

2
French
Detail of two-tiered cupboard,
*c*1590
Walnut with carving and inlays of
marble, height of cupboard 222 cm
Founders' bequest; inv.no. FW.107
The panels illustrate the Four
Elements (Air, Fire, Water and
Earth), following engravings by
Heinrich Goltzius (1558-1616).
The engraving of Fire is dated
1586, giving the earliest date for
the cupboard. Each engraving
includes a background scene of an
appropriate Biblical event, omitted
in the carvings.

3

3
French or English
Part of embroidered valance,
*c*1580
Wool and silk on linen canvas,
cross and tent stitch, height
53.5 cm
Founders' bequest;
inv.no. Emb.282b

4
**Circle of Francesco Primaticcio
(1504-1570)
Italian (Bologna)**
The Rape of Helen
Oil on canvas, 155.6 × 188.6 cm
Founders' bequest; inv.no. 76
A variant of a drawing by
Primaticcio in the Louvre, the
painting was once in the
celebrated collection of the Dukes
of Buckingham when it was
considered to be by Primaticcio
himself. John Bowes bought it as
such from Edward Solly (export
merchant and notable collector of
paintings) in 1841.

5
French
Embroidered table carpet with
biblical scenes, *c*1600
Wool and silk on linen canvas,
cross and tent stitch, 218 × 273 cm
Purchased 1989; inv.no. 1989.31

4

5

2 The Seventeenth Century

In collecting fine and decorative arts of the seventeenth century, the Bowes seem to have attempted a systematic and chronological survey, rather than to have followed particular enthusiasms. They achieved a remarkably broad spread of different types of objects. However, paintings and tapestries do feature more prominently than furniture or ceramics. This may have had more to do with price and availability than choice. Ceramics include fine Dutch tin-glazed earthenware, early products from Nevers and Rouen, and German lead-glazed wares. The piece from Rouen (p. 37) is a later addition to the collection.

There is a very good collection of Italian, Spanish, French, Dutch and Flemish paintings. The French works, from the classical nativity scene by Jacques Stella (p. 30) to a large Baroque flower painting by Jean-Baptiste Monnoyer, have a wide appeal. Some of the most enjoyable and decorative paintings in the Museum are still lifes of the seventeenth century.

Tapestries of this period are well represented. John and Josephine Bowes quickly amassed a large collection (176 pieces) ranging in date from 1500 to the 1780s and featuring all the major centres of tapestry production. Many, however, are incomplete fragments. There are two important sets from the seventeenth century. One, telling the story of Dido and Aeneas, was woven in Paris in about 1690. There is also a fine group of five pieces from a larger set telling the story of Cupid and Psyche, woven at Beauvais between 1670 and 1690. The inclusion of the Sun King's symbol on the borders has led to speculation that they belonged to Louis XIV. They hung in the principal drawing-room (Grand Salon) at Louveciennes.

Although theirs is now recognized as a major collection, and one of the largest in Britain, the Bowes appeared to buy tapestries by the metre regardless of quality or subject matter. During 1869 and 1870 they corresponded regularly (once a fortnight) with a dealer in Ghent called Rogiers and bought from him almost as regularly. The following translated excerpt, dated 12th October 1869, is typical: 'I have been offered a tapestry of three square metres in the same state as the one from Bruges but without holes, and dirtier, at the price of 60 francs (it won't stay there long).' He concludes with a bill totalling 2,517 francs which includes four tapestries at 675 F (£27), several pieces of tapestry at 26 F (£1) and one large tapestry at 135 F (£5.50). They appear to have bought most of the tapestries unseen, disregarding condition in favour of a good price. The fifty tapestries displayed during the first forty years of the Museum's public life have become very frail. The majority of the collection is now in store, in need of conservation.

Apart from a number of ecclesiastical pieces, the embroideries the Bowes collected are of a domestic nature. It is not surprising that seventeenth-century embroidery is well represented in their collection, as the technique was frequently used at that time for furnishings and to decorate household articles. The embroideries range from bed valances of canvas work to cut-work covers and gaming sacks with metal thread embroidery, mostly French in origin. The finely worked figure of Charles II was probably intended for a mirror frame and is one of a number of English pieces bought by the Bowes (p. 38). This group was augmented in the 1930s with a gift of eight pieces from Sir William Burrell. There are no examples of woven textiles or dress of this period, but the collecting of lace was taken seriously by the Bowes. The earliest pieces are from the seventeenth century and are mainly Italian. Although not of the finest quality, there are interesting examples of both furnishing and simple peasant-type laces. These were purchased almost exclusively from the dealer Lepautre in the late 1860s together with French and Flemish laces of the eighteenth and nineteenth centuries.

The Bowes's purchases of seventeenth-century French furniture were sparse, perhaps because by 1860 the best seventeenth-century cabinet-work was already fashionable and thus expensive. The Warwick Cabinet and the clock from Estonia (p. 37) illustrate the high quality of European work that has been acquired for the Museum since the 1950s. The Warwick Cabinet (p. 36) is one of the finest pieces of late seventeenth-century marquetry in existence, and has been called the masterpiece in marquetry of André-Charles Boulle. The gunstock (p. 36) is part of a large collection of woodcarvings brought together by the Bowes, presumably as an 'educational' collection for the Museum. Many of the designs on these pieces certainly derive from engraved sources. Those that have now been traced, like the *Return of the Prodigal Son* on an armchair of *c*1690 (p. 36), illustrate the way in which the richness of the collection continues to unfold.

1

**Attributed to Francesco
Fracanzano (1612-*c*1656)
Italian (Naples)**
St Paul
Oil on canvas, 235.2 × 115.6 cm
Founders' bequest; inv.no. 68

1

1
French (?)
Landscape with a town on a hill,
17th century
Oil on canvas, 106.7 × 126.4 cm
Founders' bequest; inv.no. 185
Possibly a view of a town in
Belgium, the painting, in its
emphasis on what might be called
the bone-structure of the landscape
rather than on its surface qualities,
looks forward in spirit to Corot and
Cézanne. John Bowes purchased it
in the 1840s from Edward Solly as
a work by the Dutch artist,
Willem Schellincks.

2
Jacques Stella (1596-1657)
French
The Nativity, signed and dated
1639
Oil on copper, 65.4 × 80.6 cm
Founders' bequest; inv. no. 60

3
Simon de Vlieger (*c*1600-1653)
Dutch
Dutch men-of-war at anchor,
signed, *c*1650
Oil on panel, 102.2 × 125.7 cm
Founders' bequest; inv.no. 98

4
French
Fountain mask of a river god,
*c*1650-*c*1670
Gilt-bronze, height 65 cm
Purchased 1966; inv.no. M.218
One of several masks which
originally formed part of a
fountain complex, probably at the
Château of Saint-Cloud. It
corresponds closely with masks in
designs for fountains and pavilions
published by Antoine Le Pautre
(1621-1681) between 1652 and
1653 and may possibly be the
work of the sculptor Martin
Desjardins (1640-1694).

5
North German
Pendant depicting the Emperors
Otto II (955-983) and Otto III
(980-1002), *c*1700
Carved amber, mounted in gilt
metal, height 6 cm
Founders' bequest; inv.no. X.5326
Amber is a fossil resin, derived
from conifers, found along the
shores of the Baltic Sea. It was

much used for carved ornaments
in Germany in the 17th and 18th
centuries. This piece was formerly
in the collection of Duke Anton
Ulrich of Brunswick (died 1714) or
his son August Wilhelm. It is not
known when it left the Brunswick
collection.

1

2

3

4

5

1
Juan Bautista Maíno (1581-1641)
Spanish (Toledo and Madrid)
St Agabus
Oil on canvas, 110.5 × 90.2 cm
Founders' bequest; inv.no. 807

2
Antonio de Pereda (c1608-1669)
Spanish (Madrid)
Tobias restoring his father's sight,
signed and dated 1652
Oil on canvas, 192 × 157 cm
Founders' bequest; inv.no. 34

3
Francesco Trevisani (1656-1746)
Italian (Rome)
Cardinal Pietro Ottoboni, signed,
*c*1700
Oil on canvas, 134.3 × 98.5 cm
Founders' bequest; inv.no. 70
Pietro Ottoboni, who became a
cardinal in 1689, was the most
important patron of the arts in
early 18th-century Rome,
gathering about him the most
prominent musicians (including
the young Handel), writers and
artists of his day. This portrait is a
bridge between the grand style of
Italian Baroque and later
18th-century portraiture as
typified by Pompeo Batoni.

1

2

1

2

3

1
Jacob van Hulsdonck
(1582-1647)
Flemish
Breakfast-piece, dated 1614
Oil on panel, 65.4 × 106.8 cm
Founders' bequest; inv.no. 99

2
Jacques Linard (c1600-1645)
French
Peaches, plums and melon, dated
1642
Oil on panel, 56.2 × 75.8 cm
Founders' bequest; inv.no. 1070

3
German
Model of a Nuremburg kitchen,
*c*1700
Wood with pewter and brass pots
and pans, 53 × 74 cm (model of
cook, plaster, Italian, 18th century)
Purchased 1948; inv.no. 1948.22

1

2

1
**Attributed to André-Charles
Boulle (1642-1732)**
French
Marquetry panel, *c*1690 mounted
in an English cabinet, *c*1780
Ebony and exotic woods, on a
carcase of oak, height of panel
87 cm
Purchased 1979;
inv.no. 1979.63.FW
The cabinet, attributed to Mayhew
and Ince, was built specifically to
show the earlier panel. No
documentary evidence links the
panel to Boulle, but its quality is
comparable with a well-known
group of pieces associated with his

workshop, and its size and
sophisticated design make it the
finest known panel of this group.

2
**Possibly by Johan Eberhard
Somer (fl.1650)**
French
Gunstock, *c*1640-1650
Walnut, length 38.2 cm
Founders' bequest; inv.no. X.802
A gunstock signed by Johan
Eberhard Somer, and carved with
a battle scene after an engraving
by Antonio Tempesta (1555-1630)
is in the Royal Armoury,
Stockholm. There are similarities

3

between this and The Bowes
Museum piece, where the design is
almost certainly based on another
Tempesta engraving.

3
French
Armchair, *c*1690
Frame of walnut, upholstery in
woollen embroidery on canvas,
height 114 cm
Founders' bequest; inv.no. FW.395
Such untouched survivals of early
upholstery are rare. Although this

chair never had the extravagant
fringing often found on 17th-
century furniture, the original
colours were vivid and sumptuous.
The main back panel derives from
an engraving of *The Return of the
Prodigal Son* by Antonio Tempesta
(1555-1630).

4
**Hinrich Nehring of Reval
(dates unknown)**
Estonian
Horizontal clock, signed, *c*1670
Cast of gilt-metal and silver, width
11.5 cm
Purchased 1959; inv.no. CW.82

4

5

6

7

5
**Factory of Adriaen Kocks
Dutch (Delft)**
Pair of vases painted in the
Japanese imari style, *c*1700
Tin-glazed earthenware, painted
in colours and gilt, height 28 cm
Founders' bequest;
inv.no. X.1599.1–2

6
Probably German
Tankard, engraved with scenes
depicting the dangers of love,
*c*1700
Silver, engraved and gilt, height
23 cm
Founders' bequest; inv.no. X.4606

7
French (Rouen)
Saucer, *c*1700
Soft-paste porcelain, painted in
underglaze blue, diameter 12 cm
Purchased 1988 (Enid Goldblatt
Collection); inv.no. Cer.1988.335

1

2

1
Italian (Genoa)
Long band, part of embroidered
cover, c1620
Bobbin lace and embroidered linen
with needle lace insertions,
44 × 183 cm
Founders' bequest;
inv.no. 1986.24.13

2
English
Panel embroidered with a portrait
of King Charles II, c1660
Coloured silks on satin, mainly
long and short stitch, 48.5 × 18 cm
Founders' bequest; inv.no. Emb.440

4

3

French or Italian

Figure of *St Peter* in raised-work
embroidery, late 17th century
Couched silver and silver gilt
thread and silk over padding,
frame 33.5 × 32 cm
Founders' bequest; inv.no. Emb.390

4

French

Embroidered bed tester and
valances, late 17th century
Silk satin with applied silk galloon
and cord, quilted, 194 × 167 cm,
valance height 21 cm
Founders' bequest; inv.no. Emb.248

1

**Attributed to the workshop of
Raphael de la Planche (active
1625-1661)**
French (Paris)

Tapestry, *Apollo and the Muses,*
*c*1650

Wool warp, wool and silk weft,
382.5 × 516 cm

Founders' bequest; inv.no. Tap. 32
This mythological scene set in a
fine classical border is attributed to
the workshop of Raphael de la
Planche, a famous master weaver
and the son of a Flemish weaver
brought to France by Henry IV in
1607. The gold fleur-de-lys, the
mark for Paris, is evident at the
right selvedge. In the centre of the
upper border is the coat of arms of
the Grimaldi of Monaco. The
tapestry was probably woven for
Honoré II, Prince of Monaco, who
died in 1662.

1

3 Oriental Art

The Bowes themselves made little attempt to cover the field of oriental art, the subject being too specialized and little known in mid-nineteenth-century Paris. Some fine oriental textiles, most notably a Bengal bed-hanging of the late sixteenth century, represent the East in the textiles collection. However, at the Paris Exhibition of 1867 they did buy representative specimens of woodwork, metalwork and textiles from Persia, India and Turkey, clearly in an attempt to broaden the international scope of their museum. Just before her death, Josephine Bowes seems to have acquired a few fine pieces of cabinet-work from Japan, a country which was the rage in artistic circles in the 1870s.

In 1878 John Bowes's cousin, Susan Davidson, left him her collection of over a thousand oriental ceramics, some of which may have been acquired by earlier members of the Bowes family. These cover almost every aspect of the export wares known to the Western market from the seventeenth century to the mid-nineteenth century. Most important are some rare pieces of Japanese export porcelain in the *kakiemon* and *imari* styles.

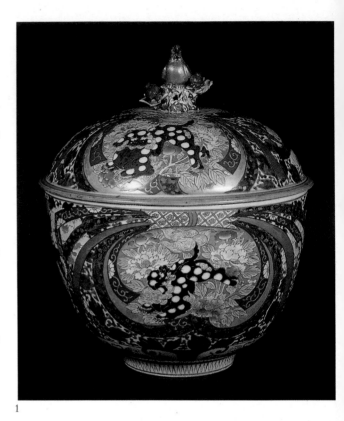

1

2

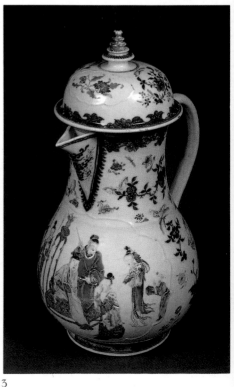

3

1

Japanese (Arita)
Bowl and cover, one of a set of
three, *c*1700
Hard-paste porcelain, painted with
imari colours and gilt, height
41 cm
Founders' bequest; inv.no. X.4491

2

Japanese (Arita)
Vase, one of a pair, *c*1680
Hard-paste porcelain, painted in
enamel colours in the *kakiemon*
style, height 36.5 cm
Founders' bequest; inv.no. X.4453

3

Chinese (Jingdezhen)
Jug and cover, one of a pair, *c*1750
Hard-paste porcelain, coloured
enamels and gold, height 40 cm
Founders' bequest; inv.no. X.5587

4

Indian for European market
Detail of embroidered fabric,
*c*1725-50
Coloured silks on glazed cotton,
chain stitch, pattern repeat 93 cm
Founders' bequest; inv.no. 1964.93b

5

Japanese
Cabinet, *c*1870
Lacquer and wood,
36 × 38.5 × 17.5 cm
Founders' bequest; inv.no. X.975

4

5

4 The Eighteenth Century

The Bowes Museum is perhaps best known for its extensive and comprehensive collection of eighteenth-century Continental fine and decorative arts. These are wide ranging and cover the field in a way unparalleled outside the National collections in London. However, in the 1860s, when John and Josephine Bowes were making their acquisitions, the eighteenth century was not generally recognized as a period worthy of consideration by museums. They thought the medieval and Renaissance periods to be of greater significance. It is part of the originality of the Bowes's museum project that they gave this century full weight.

The first eighteenth-century pieces were not collected as works of art in themselves, but formed part of the furnishings of their house on the rue de Berlin in Paris, or their country home at Louveciennes, and were supplied by Monbro fils aîné. Although many of these have suffered extensive restoration in order to make them acceptable to nineteenth-century taste, some smaller items, such as the globe clock (p. 55) are unaltered and important works of art in their own right, as well as being every-day working objects. Important French furniture, sought after by such rich connoisseurs as the Marquess of Hertford and various members of the Rothschild family, was already beyond the range of the Bowes's purse. The only pieces with a certain provenance from the royal palaces, a table from the Garde-Meuble of Marie-Antoinette and a fire-screen from the Tuileries, have been added in recent times. The most important item of eighteenth-century French furniture, a lady's writing desk by Martin Carlin (p. 55), is a recent gift from HM Government, after being accepted in lieu of capital transfer tax.

Nor were eighteenth-century paintings generally collected by museums, although works of the finest eighteenth-century painters, such as Watteau and Boucher, were already expensive by the mid-nineteenth century. The Bowes's policy of buying cheaply tended to exclude the purchase of great masterpieces, but they did succeed in buying some untypical works by fashionable artists, or masterworks by artists whose importance was not then appreciated. This accounts for the presence in the collection of a rare landscape by the French court painter François Boucher (p. 50), who is more usually associated with erotic mythological subjects, and two important oil-sketches by the Italian painters Luca Giordano and Giambattista Tiepolo (pp. 47, 45), both artists little known or appreciated a hundred years ago. Josephine Bowes's interest in landscape painting led to the acquisition of a fine series of French landscapes by Allegrain, Robert, Vernet, Genillion, Valenciennes and other French artists seldom encountered in British collections.

The Bowes continued the collection of textiles into the eighteenth century and bought many tapestries and embroideries, including some vestments. However, the majority of eighteenth-century pieces consists of embroidered and tapestry-woven chair covers (p. 56), of which the founders amassed a collection of over seven hundred. They were presumably discarded when chairs were re-upholstered in the mid-nineteenth century. Some of these may have been bought for possible reuse, as the bills from Monbro for furnishing Louveciennes refer to the re-upholstery of chairs in 'Monsieur's tapestry'. Today, however, they form an almost unique archive of late seventeenth- and eighteenth-century French furniture designs.

The collection of ceramics was particularly close to Josephine Bowes's heart and is one of the largest and most important in Britain, covering the full range of Continental porcelain and faience from medieval times to the nineteenth century. Its greatest strength is concentrated in the eighteenth century. The collections of Delftware and French and German faience – hardly collected in the 1860s – are almost unrivalled in Britain and contain many unusual or dated pieces. The collection is naturally strong in the products of the early French 'soft-paste' porcelain factories, such as Saint-Cloud, Chantilly (p. 61), Vincennes and Sèvres, although the German 'hard-paste' factories are also well represented. In general, the collection lacks the large vases and figure groups so sought after in the nineteenth century. Most of the objects are small in scale and delicate in decoration, being suited to both Josephine Bowes's exquisite taste and her limited purse. Especially characteristic of her taste is the collection of about fifty individually decorated cups and saucers from the Sèvres factory (p. 60). The Bowes were buying as much for social and historical interest as artistic, and formed parallel collections of playing cards, locks and keys, sewing accoutrements, tobacco rasps, and

1
Giovanni Battista Tiepolo
(1696-1770)
Italian (Venice)
The harnessing of the horses of the
Sun, c1731
Oil on canvas, 98.1 × 73.6 cm
Founders' bequest; inv.no. 51

Tiepolo's work in the Palazzo
Archinto in Milan, completed in
1731, was destroyed during the
Second World War. The sketch is
probably a preliminary exploration
of the theme of the ceiling, Apollo
and Phaethon, rather than an
actual *modello* for the fresco.

1

other items rarely encountered in an art museum. The collection was naturally almost devoid of English pieces, but a few examples of English pottery, porcelain and furniture came with the bequest of John Bowes's cousin, Susan Davidson, in 1878.

Although the Bowes's purchasing policy tended to rule out the acquisition of a comprehensive collection of works in precious metals, they did acquire one piece of silver of outstanding importance, which has become the Museum's best-known and best-loved object: an eighteenth-century English mechanical silver swan, which, when the mechanism is wound, bends its neck and appears to catch and swallow a fish from the water (p. 58). It was shown at the Paris International Exhibition of 1867, where it was noted by the American author Mark Twain, and was bought by John Bowes for £200 in 1872.

Apart from this, British eighteenth-century decorative arts were hardly represented among the founders' purchases. The years succeeding John Bowes's death saw the Trustees struggling to maintain the fabric of the building, which inevitably left little money for acquisitions. However, a start was made in building up a parallel collection of English works of art with gifts of English glass and embroideries by Sir William Burrell in1939 and of English porcelain by Mrs. J. H. Burn in 1950. The purchase of late seventeenth-century panelling from West Auckland Manor House, Bishop Auckland, in 1952 led to the eventual formation of a series of English period rooms from the sixteenth century to the nineteenth century. The most important of these are the long gallery from Gilling Castle, Yorkshire, and sections of the music room of Chesterfield House, London (p. 54), which enable the Museum to show the major stylistic differences between 'Palladian' and 'Rococo' in eighteenth-century Britain – the latter imported from France.

Although often seen as mere backgrounds, these are in fact important works of art in their own right, which now contain some distinguished examples of English eighteenth-century furniture. In 1961 a particularly happy purchase was Mary Eleanor Bowes's botanical cabinet, an outstanding example of Neoclassical design (p. 54), and a poignant reminder of the ill-fated lady from whom both John Bowes and the present Royal family descended. The collection of musical instruments has also been built up and put into working order, the most important item being a harpsichord by J. and A. Kirckman purchased in 1976.

A major addition to the eighteenth-century collections in the 1980s was the acquisition, through public appeal, of two large paintings by the great Venetian artist Canaletto (pp. 48–49), which had been on loan to the Museum since 1972. Fine pieces of Sèvres porcelain with rich ground colours have been added, as well as items from virtually all the eighteenth-century European factories with the purchase of the Enid Goldblatt collection in 1988 (p. 61). This large and important collection has dovetailed excellently into the existing holdings to create one of the most comprehensive groups of European porcelain in Britain, and brings The Bowes Museum's representation of eighteenth-century decorative arts to a level of international importance.

1

1

Luca Giordano (1634-1705)
Italian (Naples)
The Triumph of Judith, c1703
Oil on canvas, 71.1 × 103.5 cm
Founders' bequest; inv.no. 20
The sketch is related to a fresco of
the same subject painted on the
vault of the Cappella del Tesoro in
the Certosa di S. Martino, Naples.
The fresco was begun after the ten
years the artist had spent in Spain
and completed in 1704, the year
before he died.

1

2

1
**Giovanni Antonio Canal called
Canaletto (1697-1768)
Italian (Venice)**
Regatta on the Grand Canal, 1730s
Oil on canvas, 149.8 × 218.4 cm
Purchased 1982; inv.no. 1982.32.2
This is one of a pair of exceptional
Canalettos purchased by the
Museum in 1982 following a
nationwide fund-raising appeal.
The oarsmen in two of the
principal ornamental craft wear
blue and white. As the coat of
arms of Doge Alvise Pisani was
also blue and white, perhaps the
picture was painted during his
period of office, 1735-1741.

2
**Francesco Foschi (active
mid-18th century)
Italian (Rome)**
Snowy landscape
Oil on canvas, 96.5 × 135.3 cm
Founders' bequest; inv.no. 355

3

4

3

**Giovanni Antonio Canal called
Canaletto (1697-1768)
Italian (Venice)**
*The Bucintoro returning to the
Molo*, early 1730s.
Oil on canvas, 156.3 × 237.5 cm
Purchased 1982; inv.no. 1982.32.1
The Bucintoro was the state barge
of the Doge of Venice. It has just
returned to the Molo, the quay in
front of the Doge's Palace, after
the annual ceremony of the
Wedding of the Sea on Ascension
Day. Various ambassadorial
gondolas are in attendance. The
gondola in the foreground carries
the French Royal arms. This
suggests that the painting was
commissioned by the French
Ambassador to Venice, Jacques-
Vincent Languet, Comte de Gergy
(1667-1734).

4

**Etienne Allegrain (1653-1736)
French**
Classical landscape
Oil on canvas, 114.6 × 162.4 cm
Founders' bequest; inv.no. 338

1

François Boucher (1703-1770)
French
Landscape with water-mill, signed
and dated 1743
Oil on canvas, 90.8 × 118.1 cm
Founders' bequest; inv.no. 486

2

Hubert Robert (1733-1808)
French
Architectural capriccio with obelisk,
1768
Oil on canvas, 106 × 139.1 cm
Founders' bequest; inv.no. 273

3

Matthew Ward (dates unknown)
English
Room of panelling from the
gallery at Gilling Castle,
Yorkshire, 1748
Carved pinewood, with painted
decoration
Purchased 1962; inv.no. FW.49

2

1

1
Jean-Baptiste-François Genillion
(1750-1829)
French
View of the Seine, Paris, looking
east from the Porte St-Nicolas
towards the Pont-Neuf: morning
effect, 1772
Oil on canvas, 55.8 × 81 cm
Founders' bequest; inv.no. 331

2
Anne Vallayer-Coster
(1744-1818)
French
Portrait of an elderly woman with
her daughter, signed and dated
1775
Oil on canvas, 130.1 × 61.9 cm
Founders' bequest; inv.no. 329
Better known as a flower painter,
Vallayer-Coster was the most
renowned woman exhibiting at
the Salon before the advent of
Mme Vigée-Lebrun and Mme
Labille-Guiard in 1783. There are
several portraits in the Museum's
collection by female French artists.

2

3

4

3
French
Portrait of a man '*en robe de chambre*', 1740s
Oil on canvas, 76.2 × 61 cm
Founders' bequest; inv.no. 552

4
Circle of François Drouais (1727-1775)
French
Portrait of a child
Oil on canvas, 46.3 × 35.5 cm
Founders' bequest; inv.no. 294

5
Jean-Jacques Bachelier (1724-1806)
French
Dog of the Havana breed, signed and dated 1768
Oil on canvas, 69.8 × 91.1 cm
Founders' bequest; inv.no. 913
This is a splendid piece of rococo nonsense. Bachelier was a highly successful painter of flowers and animals. He was elected to the Académie Royale on the recommendation of Jean-Baptiste Oudry in 1750 and became director of the Vincennes-Sèvres porcelain factory in 1752, a position he held for over forty years.

5

1

1
English
Room of panelling from
Chesterfield House, London, *c*1750
Softwood and hardwoods, carved,
painted and gilded
Presented by Sir Nicholas
Williamson, 1968; inv.no. FW.37
Chesterfield House was built for
the francophile fourth Earl of
Chesterfield by the architect Isaac
Ware (*c*1707-1766). The main
panels follow closely published
designs by the French Rococo
designer Nicolas Pineau (1684-
1754). The room was altered when
it was moved in the 1930s to
Whitburn Hall, Sunderland.

2
English
Cabinet for botanical specimens,
made for Mary Eleanor Bowes,
Countess of Strathmore, *c*1780
Veneered in burr elm and
kingwood on oak, with boxwood
decoration, height 136 cm
Purchased 1961; inv.no. FW.56

3
**Possibly John Harrison
(fl.1765-1798)**
English (Newcastle)
Longcase clock, *c*1780, the
movement signed 'Harrison,
Newcastle'
Case of mahogany, height 236 cm
Founders' bequest; inv.no. CW.13

4
Jacob and Abraham Kirckman
English (London)
Keyboard from harpsichord, 1785
Case in mahogany, with veneers of
figured mahogany and satinwood,
with penwork decoration and
staining; length of harpsichord
241 cm
Purchased 1976;
inv.no. 1976.10.M.Inst.

2

5
French
Revolving-band clock, *c*1720, with 19th-century restorations; the movement is signed 'Martin à Paris'
Gilt bronze with enamelling; the plinth veneered in ebony with boule marquetry, height 65 cm
Founders' bequest; inv.no. CW.10

6
Martin Carlin (d.1785)
French (Paris)
Lady's writing table, 1765
Veneered in tulipwood on oak; mounted with Sèvres porcelain and gilt bronze. One plaque carries the Sèvres date letter and the decorator's mark of Antoine-Toussaint Cornaille (working 1755-1800); height 80.5 cm
Accepted in lieu of Capital Transfer Tax by HM Treasury, and allocated to the Museum in 1985; inv.no. 1985.4.FW
This is the earliest of eleven writing tables made to the same design between 1765 and 1774 by Martin Carlin, undoubtedly as commissions of the *marchand-mercier* Simon-Philippe Poirier.

3

4

5

6

1

English

Embroidery from a firescreen or
chairback, mid-18th century
Wool and silk on linen, tent stitch,
70 × 54 cm
Founders' bequest; inv.no. 1963.465

2

French

Embroidered chairback (one of
two pairs of matching covers)
*c*1700
Wool and silk on canvas, cross and
tent stitch, 63.5 × 50.5 cm
Founders' bequest;
inv.no. Emb.76d

3

French

Detail of man's embroidered
waistcoat, 1740-1750
Coloured silks, metal threads and
sequins on silk, length 97 cm
Purchased 1984; inv.no. 1984.8

1

2

3

1
Workshop of James Cox
English (London)
Mechanical swan, *c*1773
Silver with glass and metal
fittings, height 80 cm
Founders' bequest; inv.no. X.4653
This fine piece of silverwork is
first recorded in the Mechanical
Museum of James Cox, a London
showman and dealer, in 1774. The
swan appears to preen itself and
then bend its neck and take a fish
from the water. The works may be
by John Joseph Merlin, a famous
inventor of the time. The swan
was exhibited at the Paris
International Exhibition of 1867
and bought by John Bowes in 1872
for £200.

2
French
Firedogs, with figures of Venus
and Vulcan, *c*1740
Gilt bronze, height 42 cm
Founders' bequest; inv.no. FW.44

1

2

3

4

5

3
Thomas Hearne (1744-1817)
English
Barnard Castle, signed and dated
1788
Watercolour on paper,
25.3 × 38.7 cm
Purchased 1961; inv.no. 1060
This highly finished watercolour is
based on drawings made ten years
earlier during the artist's 1778 tour
of the region, and may well be the
Barnard Castle subject he
exhibited at the Royal Academy
in 1788. It is an accomplished
combination of the topographical
and the picturesque. The ruins of
the Norman Castle are on the
right. The medieval bridge, rebuilt
several times after floods, is still in
use today.

4
English
Doll in original sack gown and
petticoat, 1770-1780
Carved and painted wood, silk,
linen, wool, height 54 cm
Presented in memory of Miss
Monkhouse, 1937;
inv.no. 1970.187.2b

5
English
Detail of border of embroidered
panel, early 18th century
Linen in a variety of stitches,
including drawn fabric,
needlepoint fillings and raised
stitches over cord; overall size
183 × 214.5 cm
Founders' bequest; inv.no. 1968.75

1

2

3

4

German (Wallendorf)
_roup of figures representing the
our Seasons, c1780
Hard-paste porcelain, painted in
enamel colours, height 30 cm
Founders' bequest;
inv.no. X.4378-81

2
French (Sèvres)
Group of cups and saucers, some
painted with rebuses, c1780
Soft-paste porcelain, coloured
enamels and gold; average height
of cup 6 cm
Founders' bequest;
inv.nos. X.1276/X.2175/X.1270/
X.2180

3
**Factory of Francesco and
Giuseppe Vezzi
Italian (Venice)**
Bowl, c1730
Hard-paste porcelain, painted in
enamel colours, height 8.1 cm
Purchased 1988 (Enid Goldblatt
Collection); inv.no. Cer.1988.401
The Vezzi brothers obtained the
secret of making hard-paste
porcelain from a workman from
the Vienna factory in about 1720.
This bowl is painted with a scene
showing Cephalus and Aurora
after an engraving by Antonio
Tempesta (1555-1630). It is one of
a number of items from small
European factories acquired with
the Enid Goldblatt Collection in
1988.

4
French (Sèvres)
Teapot painted with peacock
feathers against a _rose_ background,
1758
Soft-paste porcelain, painted in
enamel colours and gilt, height
9.6 cm
Founders' bequest; inv.no. X.1271

5
Group of ceramics from 18th-
century factories: faience dish from
Marseilles, c1760; Meissen
porcelain vase (one of a pair),
c1730; porcelain figure of a deer
from Copenhagen, c1783;
porcelain figure of a God from
Capodimonte, Naples, c1750,
height (figure) 22.5 cm
The vase and the figure are from

5

6

the estate of the seventh Earl
Spencer and were accepted in lieu
of Capital Transfer Tax by HM
Treasury and allocated to The
Bowes Museum in 1978; the deer
was purchased in 1988 (Enid
Goldblatt Collection);
inv.nos. Cer.1978.39.2/X.1259/
Cer.1988.101/Cer.1978.39.3

6
French (Chantilly)
Group of ceramics, c1740
Soft-paste porcelain, painted in
enamel colours, height of teapoy
16.8 cm
Founders' bequest;
inv.nos. X.1320/X.1769/X.1327

7
French (Nevers)
Group showing a peepshow, c1760
Tin-glazed earthenware and
coloured enamels, height 22 cm
Founders' bequest; inv.no. X.1348

7

5 1790-1848

For the Bowes the period 1790-1848 must have held the immediate fascination that the First and Second World Wars hold for us. The bewildering series of events would still have been vivid in the minds of elderly Frenchmen, and Josephine would have been accustomed to hearing soldiers' tales from her father who had served in the National Guard. Like many of those living during the Second Empire, the Bowes showed a keen interest in the Revolution and the First Empire. France's period of cataclysm, it answered all the nation's yearnings for romance and drama, with Marie-Antoinette as tragic heroine and Napoleon as military hero, and with France dominating the European scene.

That the Bowes bought so many portraits of the period suggests that they were fascinated by its complex political history. A full-length portrait of Napoleon by Girodet (one of thirty-six versions) dominates the gallery devoted to the Revolutionary and Napoleonic periods. Alongside it are portraits of other members of his family, including Jérôme of Westphalia (p. 65), Louis, Joseph, Pauline and Madame Mère, recorded in oil or marble. The swift turns and counter-turns of events during this period were exciting and complicated, and the Bowes recorded both sides, buying also several royalist portraits, including a full length of Charles X by Gérard, and the portrait of the duchesse d'Angoulême by Gros (p. 65).

To suggest, however, that the Bowes's only interest in paintings of this period was in portraits of political figures would be quite wrong. One of the best known of the Museum's paintings from this time is Goya's *Prison scene* (p. 63), certainly a picture making a political point, but one chiefly remembered for the carefully orchestrated lighting and its mood of resigned melancholy.

The serious historical painting of the Neoclassical period is typified by the dramatic, strongly coloured canvas of *Augustus rebuking Cinna* (p. 66), while a group of landscapes by Valenciennes represent a more pastoral aspect of Neoclassicism, which clearly appealed to the Bowes. French paintings predominate in the holdings of this period, but paintings from other countries were also collected.

The fine design for a Napoleonic throne room attributed to Percier and Fontaine (p. 68), is one of the few drawings or watercolours from the original collection (though a handful of important watercolours has been acquired in recent years). This and the Italian interior (p. 72) might suggest an interest in Empire furnishings, but the Bowes bought almost no furniture of this period and only a few examples of textiles. The most splendid piece of furniture of this date in the collections, the chair by Jacob (p. 70), was acquired only in the 1960s.

However, the Bowes do seem to have shown a particular interest in clocks made between 1790 and 1820, and bought several with handsome gilt-bronze cases in the Neoclassical style. These may have had an attraction as small-scale sculpture: the dials of such clocks were frequently dwarfed by figures. Indeed clocks of all periods and several countries were bought, and this collection has been developed in this century by the addition of several handsome English clocks. Josephine may have had a personal interest in these (as she appears also to have had in sophisticated automata such as the mechanical swan) because her father was a clockmaker. Certainly, even before the Museum scheme was mooted, the clocks bought for their own domestic use were of high quality. The collection also includes a number of watches of all periods, with highly decorative casework.

An interesting minor thread of the Bowes's collecting of early nineteenth-century objects is the series of gilt-bronze pieces, not only clocks but candlesticks and a number of fine furniture mounts. Many were said to have come from the Tuileries after its destruction in 1871, but sadly it has not been possible to trace provenances for particular pieces, and one may suspect eager dealers of stretching a point.

In ceramics, this period provided rich pickings for the Bowes, from all European countries and of all qualities, from the most finished, richly coloured and finely gilded porcelains of the Vienna, Berlin and Paris factories, to the charming, naively painted *faïences patriotiques* (p. 65), of which they formed a surprisingly large collection. Symbols and slogans on these still puzzle scholars of the period. The highly sophisticated black-ground Sèvres plates dated 1791 (p. 73) epitomize the technical excellence achieved by the factory at the end of the *ancien régime*, and point forward to the strongly coloured wares of the Empire and the 1820s, which, until relatively recently, have attracted little interest from ceramics scholars though they have always been popular with the public.

1
Francisco José de Goya
(1746-1828)
Spanish (Madrid)
Prison scene
Oil on tin, 42.9 × 31.7 cm
Founders' bequest; inv.no. 29

1

In recent years the Museum has consciously acquired British art to show in parallel with the Bowes collections, and examples of ceramics and furniture range from the sixteenth to the nineteenth centuries. The 1960s saw the acquisition of the monumental lights from Northumberland House (p. 74). New British pieces are added regularly to the collection, but its basic character as a collection of continental European arts in Britain remains dominant.

In 1982 the Museum was pleased to receive from the Treasury (which had received it in lieu of capital taxes) the allocation of part of the important Regency silver made by Paul Storr, in about 1810, for the Marquess of Ormonde. This was particularly welcome as the Bowes themselves collected almost no silver (possibly considering it too expensive a purchase on their careful budget).

A more recent purchase, of two Turner watercolours (one on p. 69) was also in a field not sought after by the Bowes. Perhaps the difficulty of displaying drawings and watercolours was a deterrent, or they may have felt them insufficiently showy. In buying these two views of Gibside the Museum has sought not only to strengthen its British holdings, but also to preserve an element of family history.

1
François-Joseph Kinsoen
(1770-1839)
French
Jérôme Bonaparte, King of Westphalia, after 1806
Oil on canvas, 224.2 × 145.4 cm
Founders' bequest; inv.no. 472

2
Baron Antoine-Jean Gros
(1771-1835)
French
The Duchesse d'Angoulême, signed, 1817
Oil on canvas, 73 × 60.9 cm
Founders' bequest; inv.no. 303

3
French (Nevers)
Plate painted with a scene depicting the execution of Louis XVI, 1793
Tin-glazed earthenware, painted in colours, diameter 22 cm
Founders' bequest; inv.no. X.1407

4
Baron François-Joseph Bosio
(1768-1845)
French
Charles X, King of France, after 1823
Bronze, height 76.8 cm
Founders' bequest; inv.no. S.104

1

2

3

4

1

1
Etienne-Jean Delécluze
(1781-1863)
French
The Emperor Augustus rebuking
Cornelius Cinna for his treachery,
signed and dated 1814
Oil on canvas, 215.3 × 262.9 cm
Founders' bequest; inv.no. 367
This typically Neoclassical
painting illustrates an episode
from Corneille's tragedy *Cinna*, in
which Augustus accuses Cinna of
plotting treason, saying: *Ecoute*
cependant, et tiens mieux ta
parole,/Tu veux m'assassiner
demain au Capitole.
Delécluze was a favourite pupil of
Jacques-Louis David and his first
biographer as well as a notable art
critic.

2

66

3

2
**Pierre-Henri de Valenciennes
(1750-1819)
French**
Mercury and Argus, signed and
dated 1793 (?)
Oil on panel, 24.5 × 32.4 cm
Founders' bequest; inv.no. 437

3
**François-Marius Granet
(1775-1849)
French**
Reading lesson in a convent, signed
and dated 1810
Oil on canvas, 99 × 76.8 cm
Founders' bequest; inv.no. 500

1
**Charles Percier (1764-1838) and
Pierre Fontaine (1762-1853)**
French
*Drawing for a throne room, c*1810
Pen and wash on paper,
44.7 × 54 cm
Founders' bequest; inv.no. 1050

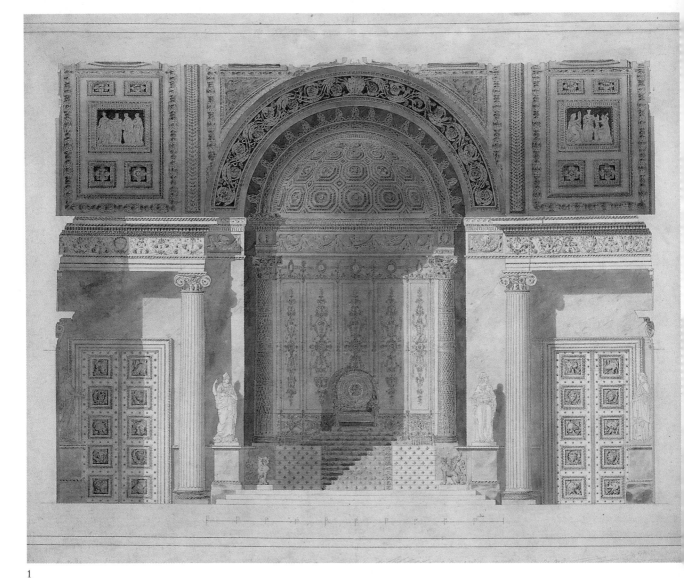

1

2
**Joseph Mallord William Turner
(1775-1851)**
English
*Gibside from the north, c*1817
Watercolour on paper,
27.4 × 45.1 cm
Purchased 1984; inv.no. 1985.10
This watercolour with its pendant,
a view from the south, was
acquired directly from the artist by
the tenth Earl of Strathmore,
father of John Bowes. Gibside

Estate had been the property of
the Bowes family since the early
18th century. Near the centre of
the watercolour, on high ground, is
Gibside Hall itself, now an empty
shell.

3
**Achille-Etna Michallon
(1796-1822)**
French
After the thunderstorm, signed and
dated 1817

Oil on canvas, 79.3 × 99.1 cm
Founders' bequest; inv.no. 348
Michallon showed early talent: he
exhibited at the Salon when he
was only sixteen. It was predicted
that he would become a 'modern
Poussin'. However, his promising
career was tragically cut short by
his death at the early age of
twenty-six. He was Corot's first
master. The painting is one of a
pendant pair.

2

3

1

2

3

1
Attributed to Antoine-André Ravrio (1759-1814)
French
Clock, c1810
Gilt-bronze, the movement is an English replacement, height 53 cm
Founders' bequest; inv.no. CW.46

2
Georges Jacob (1739-1814)
French
Armchair for the Hôtel Marbeuf, Paris, c1790
Beechwood, painted and gilded; the upholstery modern, height 96 cm
Purchased 1969; inv.no. FW.359
A label on this chair reads 'Madame la Marquise de Marbeuf, Chambre à Coucher'. The Hôtel

Marbeuf in Paris was redecorated in 1790 under the direction of Jean-Démosthène Dugourc (1749-1825). The chair reflects Dugourc's bold and severe Neoclassicism, foreshadowing the Empire style.

3
French
Candlestick with inventory mark of the Elysée Palace, Empire period, 1804-1815
Ormolu, height 27 cm
Founders' bequest; inv.no. M.227

4
German (probably Hamburg)
Secretaire, c1845
Mahogany, height 200 cm
Purchased 1962; inv.no. FW.190

1
Pietro Nocchi (d. c1855)
Italian (Lucca)
Lady with a harp lute, signed and
dated 1811
Oil on canvas, 59.7 × 48.2 cm
Founders' bequest; inv.no. 876

2
Jean-Pierre Dantan (1800-1869)
French
Caricature: statuette of the *Dukes
of Cumberland and Gloucester*,
signed and dated 1834
Plaster of Paris, height 33.2 cm
Founders' bequest; inv.no. S.126

3
Bissardon, Cousin et Bony
French (Lyons)
Detail of woven furnishing
brocade and separate border,
probably from the Palais des
Tuileries, 1811-1813
Satin brocaded with coloured silks,
pattern repeat 99 cm
Founders' bequest; inv.no. Tex.18

4
French (Sèvres)
Plate, 1791
Soft-paste porcelain, painted in
enamel colours and decorated with
two colours of gold and platinum,
diameter 22.4 cm
Founders' bequest; inv.no. X.1291.3
The decoration reproduces the
effect of oriental lacquer. One of a
set of six plates in the Museum
from a service sold to the
unfortunate M. de Semonville,
French Ambassador to the Court of
Turin (which refused to receive
him) and later to the Court of
Constantinople (which he did not
reach, as he was captured by the
Austrians and imprisoned).

5
French (Paris)
Pattern plate, c1810
Hard-paste porcelain, painted in
enamel colours and gilt, diameter
24.3 cm
Founders' bequest; inv.no. X.2496

1

2

3

4

5

1

1
William Collins (active 1812-1823)
English
Pair of gas-lights supplied for Northumberland House, London, 1823
Lacquered brass; the globes added later, height 310 cm
Purchased 1960; inv.no. FW.71
In 1823 William Collins presented a bill to the Duke of Northumberland for 'The Grand Staircase Railing' and '2 large Candelabra' for Northumberland House. The cost was £2000. They were described as of 'Grecian Metal', with a lacquered surface in place of gilding.

2
Firm of Farrington
English (Newcastle)
Cellaret for Hoppyland Hall, County Durham, c1810
Mahogany with gilded and painted details including the arms of Leyton-Blenkinsopp, height 80 cm
Bequeathed by Mrs Dowling, 1952; inv.no. FW.75

2

3
Paul Storr (1771-1844)
English (London)
Vegetable dish and cover, 1808
Silver, cast and chased, the stand of Sheffield plate, height 27.5 cm
Allocated by HM Treasury, 1982; inv.no. Sil.1982.24.5
One of a pair. The dish forms part of a large collection of Regency silver from the estate of the sixth Marquess of Ormonde, accepted in lieu of capital transfer tax by HM Treasury and allocated to The Bowes Museum in 1982.

3

4
Possibly Swiss
Mechanical mouse, c1810
Gold with seed pearls and garnet eyes, length (including tail) 11 cm
Founders' bequest; inv.no. X.5447
One of a number of mechanical items in the museum. Bought by Josephine Bowes from the London dealer P. Albert for £33 on 12 May 1871, when the couple were in London, sheltering from the siege of Paris. (The item may have had a special significance for them, as John called Josephine 'Puss'.)

4

6 1848-1880

In part, the contemporary collections for the Museum were made unconsciously in the ten years before the museum project was formally adopted by the Bowes. The large collection of furniture of the Second Empire period, for which the Museum is now well known and which is a collection unique of its type in Britain, was acquired in the 1850s by John and Josephine for their houses, mostly for the château at Louveciennes and the house in rue de Berlin, Paris. When the museum project began to take over as their primary goal, Louveciennes was sold up and in 1862 the contents were packed into cases and sent to Streatlam Castle. In 1882 the cases were transferred to the Museum together with the many more which contained actual exhibits. To the early trustees, of course, most of this furniture was an embarrassment. Some was optimistically catalogued as the 'Louis XV' or 'Louis XVI' which it copied, but what could not be argued back into a more respectable century received apology or explanation in catalogues rather than celebration. In 1917 some was even sold at auction.

It was not until the 1960s that the collection was once again reassessed. At that time nineteenth-century decorative arts were just beginning to attract serious scholarly attention, and The Bowes Museum's Second Empire furnishings were at last recognized as a collection rare in Britain. Not only had a large part of the decorative schemes for two houses survived, but the documentation had survived also. A large number of bills for the furnishings, from the Parisian firm of Monbro fils aîné, still exist in the Museum archive. As a result it is possible to discover the original price of many pieces and to work out where they stood. As the discipline of furniture studies developed in the 1970s scholars also became interested in the decoration of rooms, and in the wall treatments and draperies used with different styles of furniture.

In the early 1980s the galleries of nineteenth-century French decorative arts at The Bowes Museum were entirely redisplayed, and their own furnishings formed a major part of the exhibits. The Bowes closely followed the fashions of their time, rather than showing a particularly advanced taste. Historical styles were everywhere the accepted form, the masculine side of a house (library, dining-room, billiards room) treated in the earlier styles of Louis XIII or Louis XIV in carved oak,

ebonized wood or dark boulle marquetry, the feminine side (salons, boudoirs, bedrooms) in Louis XV or Louis XVI style in giltwood or exotic veneer. The Bowes duly furnished the Louveciennes dining-room in sombre carved oak, while the Salon Bleu at rue de Berlin was hung with dark blue damask and furnished with chairs and a sofa in kingwood, in Louis XVI style.

Certain idiosyncrasies are apparent. The Bowes seem to have had a special fondness for the rather showy boulle marquetry, used in the salon at Louveciennes as well as in the library or smoking-room. The appearance in the bills of certain designated 'antique' pieces may have heralded a particular interest of the Bowes, but their presence may be incidental, a normal part of the provision by a firm which had started off very much as an antique dealer. Certainly the bills include the supply of a great deal of antique textile, the cleaning of tapestry and the re-covering of furniture using older tapestries. Three rooms on the first floor of the Museum are now dedicated to the Bowes's own furnishings.

The Bowes were even more determined as patrons of living artists. John Bowes's first essays at collecting paintings in the 1830s and 1840s had included works by J. F. Herring senior. Josephine's own skill as an artist was notable (p. 81) and she took lessons with Karl Kuwasseg. Cals painted Kuwasseg, and it may be because of this that Josephine acquired his painting of peasants (p. 80). Most of the nineteenth-century French paintings seem to have been bought from auction rather than directly from the ateliers of the artists, but occasionally there is evidence of a closer connection between artist and patron: a Gudin is labelled 'Offert à Madame Bowes'.

The collection contains many fine paintings of the Realist school. The Museum is often asked if it shows French Impressionists. Josephine Bowes died in1874, the year of the first Impressionist exhibition, and after her death John Bowes bought very few exhibits for the Museum. Instead Josephine collected attractive works by her contemporaries. Some have been out of fashion until recent years, when artists such as Bonvin (p. 84) have undergone a reappraisal. Certain pictures, such as the Courbet (p. 83) and the Fantin-Latour (p. 79), have always been popular, but others such as the Monticelli (p. 84), which was one of the most advanced and controversial pictures bought by the Bowes, spent many

1
Monbro fils aîné
French (Paris)
One of a pair of cabinets, *c*1855
Veneered in ebony and boulle
marquetry, with plaques of tin-
glazed earthenware, gilt-bronze
mounts and hardstones; brand
mark; height 163 cm
Founders' bequest; inv.no. FW.104

1

years languishing in store. Whereas the Bowes bought many portraits of political figures of the early nineteenth century, the period after 1848 was too close to their own time to allow such a choice of 'illustration'. However, exceptions are the series of paintings of events during the 1848 Revolution (p. 82) and portraits by J. D. Court.

In 1867 Paris was host to one of the series of large International Exhibitions in the late nineteenth century, and the Bowes joined the crowds thronging to it. The laying of the foundation stone of the museum was still two years away, but by 1867 the project was already in mind, and its scale was becoming demanding. A great deal would be needed to fill these grand suites of rooms. Inspired by the educational zeal of such institutions as the South Kensington Museum in London, John and Josephine bought what now seems a very bizarre group of items representing the current arts and manufactures not just of European countries but of Persia and India, Algeria and Turkey. Some of the items can never be much more than dismal curios, like the long series of carved wooden spoons or examples of cheap, utilitarian glassware from Romania. A sudden and unwise attack of economy seems to have held them in its grip. The cheapest piece, a pressed-glass salt-cellar from Sweden, cost only 35 centimes (about 1 pence). By the time the Bowes returned to the next International Exhibition, in London in 1871, their cultural course had steadied. The pieces they bought on this occasion were of notably higher quality. Ceramics and glass dominated and purchases included the Salviati glass from Venice (p. 89), a monumental vase from Berlin (p. 91) and assorted ceramics from countries as widespread as Portugal, Hungary and Denmark (p. 90), all of the highest quality. A comprehensive display of these is shown on the first floor of the Museum.

It was through the 1871 exhibition that Josephine Bowes embarked on one of her most interesting commissions, a set of glassware from the young Emile Gallé (p. 88), with whom she maintained a correspondence. This points to where her taste might have been going, as does the acquisition of tile panels in the new 'aesthetic' taste by Simpson & Co of London (p. 90). Her early death in 1874 left these as isolated experiments.

1
Henri Fantin-Latour
(1836-1904)
French
Fruit and flowers, signed and
dated 1866
Oil on canvas, 60 × 44.1 cm
Founders' bequest; inv.no. 514

1

1
**Charles-Emile Jacque
(1813-1894)**
French
Mowers, signed, before 1869
Oil on panel, 27.3 × 21.9 cm
Founders' bequest; inv.no. 735

2
Adolphe-Felix Cals (1810-1880)
French
Peasant woman and child, signed
and dated 1846
Oil on canvas, 46.4 × 37.8 cm
Founders' bequest; inv.no. 647

3
Josephine Bowes (1825-1874)
French
Snow scene in the South of France,
signed, datable from 1868
Oil on canvas, 131 × 185.3 cm
Founders' bequest; inv.no. J.22
Josephine Bowes was co-founder of
The Bowes Museum. She was a
highly competent amateur painter,
well able to work convincingly on
a large scale, as this picture shows.
Her work, in the Realist style, was
accepted on several occasions for
exhibition at the Salon. From
1868, after she became Countess of
Montalbo, she signed herself
'Josephine M. Bowes'.

1

2

3

1

2

3

1
**Eugène-Louis Boudin
(1825-1908)
French**
Beach scene at low tide, signed and
dated 1867
Oil on panel, 31.1 × 47.9 cm
Founders' bequest; inv.no. 689
This beach is on the Normandy
coast. Boudin established his
reputation as a fashionable painter
with atmospheric open-air works
like this, in which he observes the
manners and dress of the upper
classes. One of the major
forerunners of Impressionism, he
was considered by Claude Monet
to have been his first master.

2
**François-Claudius Compte-Calix
(1813-1880)
French**
*Madame de Lamartine adopting
the children of patriots killed at the
barricades in Paris during the
Revolution of 1848*, signed and
dated 1848
Oil on canvas, 81.3 × 99.3 cm
Founders' bequest; inv.no. 470

3
**Gustave Courbet (1819-1877)
French**
View at Ornans, signed and dated
1864
Oil on canvas, 86.3 × 129.5 cm
Founders' bequest; inv.no. 531

1

2

3

1
**Adolphe-Joseph-Thomas
Monticelli (1824-1886)**
French
Landscape with figures and goats,
before 1866
Oil on panel, 59.4 × 40 cm
Founders' bequest; inv.no. 391
When Josephine Bowes died in
February 1874, the Impressionists
had not yet held their first
exhibition. However, in 1865, she
had bought this advanced work by
Monticelli after the dealer Lamer
had drawn her attention to it as:
'un tableau de Monticelli très
soigné. Veuillez, Madame,
l'observer, l'artiste est un garçon
qui a de l'avenir'.

2
François Bonvin (1817-1887)
French
Self-portrait, signed and dated
1847
Oil on canvas, 65.4 × 54.3 cm
Founders' bequest; inv.no. 444

3
**Auguste-Paul-Charles Anastasi
(1820-1889)**
French
The Cabaret Maurice at Bougival,
before 1874
Oil on board, 25.4 × 35.6 cm
Founders' bequest; inv.no. 724

4
Monbro fils aîné
French (Paris)
One of a pair of Candelabra,
supplied *c*1855 for the Château
Du Barry
Hard-paste porcelain, gilt-bronze
mounts, height 137 cm
Founders' bequest; inv.no. X.4431

5
James Pradier (1792-1852)
French
*Sappho, Ancient Greek writer of
lyric poetry,* 1848
Silver, height 86 cm
Founders' bequest; inv.no. M.234
This stylishly elegant statue
represents Sappho as poetess and
tormentedly brooding lover with
appropriate attributes: two billing
doves, myrtle leaves, ewer and
libation cup, lyre and a scroll
inscribed in Greek with the last
stanza of her 'Ode to Aphrodite'.
Louise Colet, the French writer,
was the model for this figure.

6
**G. Lemonnier (d. 1882) and
Charles-Martial Bernard
(1824-1896)**
French (Paris)
Snuff-boxes, *c*1860 and 1853
Gold, coloured enamels and
precious stones. Right-hand box
2.2 × 8 × 0.5 cm
Founders' bequest;
inv.nos. X.5465/X.5463

4

5

6

1
Monbro fils aîné
French (Paris)
Armchair for the Salon Bleu at
7 rue de Berlin, Paris, 1855
Veneered in kingwood with gilt-
bronze mounts; the tapestry 18th-
century Beauvais; height 97 cm
Founders' bequest; inv.no. FW.93

1

2

2
Monbro fils aîné
French (Paris)
Secretaire, c1855
Veneered in kingwood with
marquetry of several woods; gilt-
bronze mounts; height 118 cm
Founders' bequest; inv.no. FW.95

3
Debain of Paris (mechanism),
Monbro fils aîné (case)
French (Paris)
Piano-cum-harmonium, c1855,
probably made for rue de Berlin
Veneered in ebony with boulle
marquetry, height 116 cm
Founders' bequest;
inv.no. M.Inst.39
When Josephine Bowes ordered
this instrument the harmonium
was a new and fashionable
invention for which serious
composers were to write. The
combined instrument was even
more revolutionary. Josephine

3

clearly valued it. The expensive
casing here includes the Bowes
arms, and she accorded a piano the
same decoration.

4
Monbro fils aîné
French (Paris)
Wardrobe, c1855

Veneered in tulipwood with panels
of marquetry incorporating metal
and horn; gilt-bronze mounts;
height 269 cm
Founders' bequest; inv.no. FW.110

4

1

2

3

4

1
Emile Gallé (1846-1904)
French (Nancy)
Cabaret set, *c*1872
Cut and engraved glass, height of
decanter 24.8 cm
Founders' bequest; inv.nos. G.114/
G.327/G.371/G.433
Josephine Bowes met the young
Emile Gallé at the London
International Exhibition of 1871
and commissioned a cabaret set
from him. This is his first known
commission for glass, and pre-
dates his work in the Art Nouveau
style by twenty years. Some
charming letters relating to the
commission survive in the
Museum's archive.

2
Attributed to Karl Pföhl
(1826-1894)
Bohemian
Glass, *c*1855
Glass, with amber stained overlay,
cut and engraved with a horse, and
the Bowes coat of arms on the
reverse; height 17 cm
Founders' bequest; inv.no. G.286.1
The art of cutting overlay glass
(where an outer layer of stained
glass was cut away to show clear
glass underneath) developed
rapidly in Bohemia in the 19th
century.

3
Russia
Group of objects bought from the
Paris International Exhibition
1867
Left to right: a panel carved by the
monks of Troiza-Sergui, near
Moscow, a paperweight of carved
hardstones, a glass vase enamelled
with traditional Russian figures
and a painted papier-mâché cigar
case
Height of vase 24.7 cm
Founders' bequest; inv.nos. G.375/
W.133/X.5489/S.120

4
Selection of books from the Library
Founders' bequest; unnumbered
John Bowes inherited the library
of John Davidson of Newcastle.
This was augmented by the
Bowes's own large French library
and by bindings and rarities
bought with the Museum in mind.
Latterly, the trustees have added
an important collection of volumes
on regional history.

5
Firm of Salviati
Italian (Venice)
Glass group (Paris International
Exhibition 1867)
Height of decanter 26.5 cm
Founders' bequest; inv.nos. G.378/
G.85/G.87/G.95

6
Monbro fils aîné
French (Paris)
Vitrine and clock for the dining-
room at the Château Du Barry,
*c*1854
Vitrine of carved oak; clock in gilt
and patinated bronze; height of
vitrine 152 cm
Founders' bequest; inv.no. FW.180

5

6

89

1

2

3

1
Hungarian (Herend)
Dish in imitation of Japanese
lacquer (London International
Exhibition 1871)
Hard-paste porcelain, enamel
colours and gilt, diameter 44 cm
Founders' bequest; inv.no. X.1879

2
**Firm of Simpson and Co
English (London)**
Pair of tile panels (London
International Exhibition 1871)
Lead-glazed earthenware, painted
in colours, height 109 cm
Founders' bequest;
inv.no. Cer.1991.18.1-2
Towards the end of the 19th
century, there was a reaction in
England against the flamboyant
nature of much 19th-century
design, and a more restrained style
took its place. The movement,
today termed the 'Aesthetic'
movement, was based on the
parallel influences of William
Morris and Japanese art. This pair
of 'Art Tyle Panels' was bought by
Josephine Bowes from the London
1871 Exhibition for £10.10.0d.

3
Swedish (Rörstrand)
Teaset painted with Swedish
traditional costumes (Paris
International Exhibition 1867)
Hard-paste porcelain, coloured
enamels, height of teapot 17 cm
Founders' bequest; inv.no. X.1508

4
German (Berlin)
Vase, painted with the figures of
Mercury and Hebe (London
International Exhibition 1871)
Hard-paste porcelain, painted in
enamel colours, height 87 cm
Founders' bequest; inv.no. X.4416

4

7 The Later Collections

It has been seen that additions have been made to the founders' collection, but they have not passed beyond the date of John Bowes's death in 1885. While these acquisitions have reinforced the Museum's position as the premier collection of Continental art in the North of England, other collections have also been formed in new areas and continuing in date into the twentieth century. These are costume, toys and dolls, and folk life. Their growth has very much depended on gifts from local sources, resulting in a more regional emphasis.

The costume collection is strongest in women's dress, with examples of *haute couture* from the 1860s to the 1960s (p. 95). There is a focus on dress of the mid-nineteenth century as a reflection of the world of Josephine Bowes (p. 95). Regrettably, her own wardrobe does not survive, though bills in the archives reveal that she spent astonishing amounts on her dress. These tantalizing documents are complemented by her fashion journals, now in the Museum library, which provided her with illustrations of the latest French fashions (p. 95). The collection of this period is further strengthened by costume items worn by Empress Eugénie of France, given by a local benefactor, Miss Alice Edlestone, who bought from the sale of the Empress's effects at Farnborough in 1920.

There is a notable collection of dolls, including two from the eighteenth century (p. 59), and dolls' houses.

The earliest is a model of a Nuremburg kitchen (p. 35) but there are good nineteenth- and early twentieth-century examples.

The painting of sheep-shearers (p. 92) illustrates the Museum's role in preserving aspects of Teesdale life. The folk-life collection includes vernacular furniture, topographical prints, photographs and evidence of the local nineteenth-century carpet-weaving and lead-mining industries. The tradition of quilting in the North of England is well represented by a large group of quilted and pieced bedcovers (p. 94).

The Museum also has a large and growing archaeology collection. The decision to collect local archaeological items was made in the 1920s and the Museum is now the principal archaeological repository for County Durham. This collection, which includes material from salvage and research excavations as well as chance finds, covers all periods of human history from the Middle Stone Age to the nineteenth century.

The founders themselves collected archaeological and geological specimens. They intended that their Museum, given to the people of Teesdale, should be developed in other directions. However, these later developments will never overshadow John and Josephine Bowes's personal achievement of providing an exceptional Museum of the fine and decorative arts.

1

1
**John T. Young Gilroy
(1898-1985)
English**
Sheep-shearing in Baldersdale,
*c*1949
Oil on canvas, 101.5 × 127 cm
Bequeathed by Mrs Olive Field,
1974; inv.no. 1974.57
John Gilroy was a notable
portraitist of royalty and other
prominent figures. However, he is
best known in the popular mind
for his commercial work, in
particular his advertisements for
Guinness and for Johnnie Walker
whisky. Gilroy visited Teesdale to
paint portraits, but made other
paintings, including this work.
Baldersdale meets Teesdale at
Cotherstone, a few miles west of
Barnard Castle.

2
**Liberty of London, possibly to a
design by Leonard F. Wyburd
English**
Music cabinet, *c*1897
Mahogany, with marquetry of
several woods, height 145 cm
Purchased 1962; inv.no. FW.225

2

1
Rebecca Temperley (active 1860)
English (Allendale, Northumberland)
Quilt, c1860
Plain and printed cottons, hand-sewn and quilted, 274.5 × 274.5 cm
Presented by Mrs Parker, 1964;

inv.no. 1964.517
A bordered design which incorporates piecing and appliqué with traditional North-Country quilting patterns. The border has a 'lined twist', quatrefoil hearts and leaf patterns.

2
English (Weardale, County Durham)
Quilt, mid-19th century
Pieced block design in three printed cottons, piped edges, hand-sewn and quilted, 222 × 244 cm

1

2

3

3

Bequeathed by Mrs M. Rogers,
1990; inv.no. 1990.10.1

3A
Norman Hartnell (1901-1979)
English
Detail of wedding dress and train,
1928
Silk satin and silk net embroidered
with silver lace, bugle beads and
pearls; back length 128 cm,
circumference of hem 381 cm,
train 295 × 121 cm
Presented by Mrs J. Ropner, 1981;
inv.no. 1981.8.1
Hartnell's first major successes
were designs for exquisite
weddings dresses like this for the
cream of society in the late 1920s.
This is a romantic creation with
deep medieval-style sleeves. The
graduating design of flowers on
the drop-waisted skirt is echoed in
satin on the train. The headdress is
in the form of a tiara of silver lace
and diamante.

3B
Photographic portrait of the bride,
Miss Joan Redhead, daughter of
Lady Lacon, who married Mr
J. R. Ropner at St Margaret's
Westminster on 24 July 1928
Unnumbered

4
Madame Elise, Royal
Dressmaker to the Princess of
Wales
English (London)
Woman's dress, 1868-1870
Watered silk trimmed with gold
braid, length (back) 218 cm,

circumference of hem 504 cm
Purchased 1987; inv.no. 1987.24.1

5
Fashion plates and dress bills
belonging to Josephine Bowes,
1860-1869
Founders' bequest; unnumbered

5

4

6

6
Jeanne Menault (active 1920s)
French (Paris)
Woman's hat in marquetry, c1925
Kingwood and boxwood, leather
trimming, height 17 cm
Presented by Fenwick Ltd 1964;
inv.no. 1964.700

Further Reading

Charles E. Hardy, *John Bowes and The Bowes Museum*, 1970 (and several subsequent editions)
Eric Young, *Catalogue of Spanish and Italian Paintings*, 1970
The Bowes Museum, *Short Guide*, 1985
The Bowes Museum, *John Bowes, Mystery Man of The British Turf*, 1985
Eric Young, *Catalogue of Spanish Paintings in The Bowes Museum*, 2 ed., rev. 1988
Ralph Arnold, *The Unhappy Countess*, 1957 (2 ed. 1987)

Index of Illustrations